A Place Called Home

by Alice Julia

illustrated by
Marie Garafano

W9-BDM-788

Harcourt

Orlando   Boston   Dallas   Chicago   San Diego

Visit *The Learning Site!*

www.harcourtschool.com

Earth's Geography

Have you ever seen a mountain? An ocean?
A desert? These are only a few of the features
that make up Earth's geography. A region's
geography is its natural features. Natural
features include land forms and bodies of water.

Imagine looking at Earth from the window of
a spaceship. What would Earth look like from
outer space? Then imagine looking down from
an airplane. What features would you see? Now
imagine that you are traveling by train or car.
How would the view of Earth be different?

Continents and Oceans

Imagine again that you are looking at Earth from outer space. You see large masses of land on Earth's surface. These land masses are called continents.

There are seven continents: Europe, Asia, Africa, North America, South America, Australia, and Antarctica. Continents usually are divided into smaller areas called countries.

From your view in outer space, you see that the continents are surrounded by water. These bodies of water are called oceans. An ocean is a large body of salt water. Oceans cover seventy-five percent of Earth's surface! These large bodies of water are sometimes called seas.

There are five oceans: the Atlantic, the Pacific, the Indian, the Arctic, and the Antarctic Oceans.

Islands and Peninsulas

From your spaceship view, you may also see islands. An island is a land mass surrounded by water. Islands are smaller than continents. There are many islands on Earth, including the Hawaiian Islands and the Solomon Islands.

A peninsula is like an island. But a peninsula is not completely surrounded by water. A peninsula is a piece of land nearly surrounded by water and joined to a larger land mass. The country of Italy and the state of Florida are peninsulas.

Florida

Arcti

North
America

Island

Continent

Pacific Ocean

Atlantic Ocean

South
America

Antarctic

Antarctica

Ocean

Europe

Asia

Sea

Peninsula

Africa

Continent

Australia

Indian Ocean

Ocean

Ocean

7

Mountains and Valleys

Mountain

Imagine that you are looking at Earth from an airplane. Now you have a closer view of Earth's geography. You may see a mountain as you look down. A mountain is a land form that is taller than a hill.

Sometimes mountains are grouped together. These chains of mountains are called mountain ranges. There are many mountain ranges, including the Rocky Mountains, the Alps, the Himalayas, and the Andes. On some maps and globes, mountain ranges appear as raised areas.

A valley is a low area between mountains or hills. A valley can be long or short, wide or narrow, and deep or shallow.

Valleys are formed in different ways. A valley can form when a glacier moves through a region.

Valley

A glacier is a large mass of ice. Valleys can also form when a stream or a river winds its way over the land. The water of a stream or river can wash away the soil and rocks to make a flat area.

Rivers and Streams

A river is a body of running water that forms when rain or melted snow flows over the land, making a path or channel. These channels are called river beds. Some large rivers are the Rio Grande, the Mississippi, the Congo, the Ganges, the Nile, and the Amazon.

Rivers are fed by smaller bodies of running water. These are called streams or creeks. Smaller streams and creeks may dry up during times of little rain or snow.

Lake

River

Lakes and Ponds

A lake is a body of fresh water or salt water surrounded by land. Many lakes form when rivers flow into a region and fill up low areas. Some lakes form when water fills a hollow area left by a glacier. Other lakes form when underground springs or streams come up through Earth's surface.

There are many large lakes in the world, including the Great Lakes of North America. The Great Lakes are Lake Huron, Lake Ontario, Lake Michigan, Lake Erie, and Lake Superior.

A pond is smaller and more shallow than a lake. A pond may dry up when there is no supply of water.

Stream

Deserts and Prairies

Imagine that you are looking at Earth from the window of a car or train. Now you have a close view of Earth's geography. You may see a desert from your window. A desert is a very dry region. A desert can be hot and sandy. A desert can be cold and rocky. There is very little water in a desert. Deserts have special plants that can survive the dry conditions.

There are several large deserts in the world, including the Gobi and the Sahara.

A prairie is a region of flat land covered by grass. Prairies have few trees, but they usually have dark, fertile soil. A prairie might also be called a plain.

There are few prairies in the world. The Pampas in the country of Argentina is a prairie. Another prairie is the Canterbury Plains of New Zealand. The largest prairie in the world is in central North America.

Maps and Globes

You don't have to fly in a spaceship or an airplane or ride in a car or a train to see the geography of Earth. You can use a map or a globe.

A map is a drawing of a region. A map can show continents and bodies of water. It can also show countries and states. Some maps show mountain ranges, lakes, and rivers. Special maps show deserts and prairies.

Map

Globe

A globe is similar to a map. A globe is a map that has been drawn or printed on a sphere. A globe is rounded like Earth's surface. This lets you see Earth in its actual shape.

There are globes of the sky, too. These globes show the stars and constellations as seen from Earth. There are also globes of the Moon that show its geography and regions.

A map or a globe is an easy way to explore Earth without leaving home. You can see the continent of Antarctica or the Indian Ocean. You can see the island of Fiji or the Cascade Mountains. You can see the Yukon River or Lake Victoria.

The geography of Earth is very interesting. There are so many things to see! What features of Earth have you seen? What features would you like to see?